Mind Workout for
Gifted Kids

Mind workout for
Gifted Kids

COLLINS & BROWN

First published in Great Britain in 2005 by Collins & Brown Ltd

The Chrysalis Building,

Bramley Road,

London W10 6SP

An imprint of **Chrysalis** Books Group plc

Editor: Victoria Alers-Hankey

Design: Clare Barber

This book has been completed with the help of others with whom we are

exeptionally grateful.

10 9 8 7 6 5 4 3 2 1

British Library Cataloguing-in-Publication Data:

A catalogue record for this book is available from the British Library.

ISBN 1 84340 284 X

Colour reproduction by Anorax Imaging Ltd

Printed and bound by CT Printing, China

contents

Introduction

The terms 'gifted', 'bright', 'intelligent', 'able' and 'talented' are heard everyday. They can mean different things, however, to different people.

Few children are equally 'gifted' in all areas; most have marked aptitudes in one or more fields. If you want to look at the national picture, think of your child as placed along a continuum:

1   5

1 = Average

2 = More able (top 10% of the country's children)

3 = Very able (top 5-10% of the country's children)

4 = Exceptionally able (top 2% of the country's children)

5 = Genius (one or two children in the whole of the UK)

It is clear that children who are more able will have special needs in the same way as those children who have learning difficulties and will need support and challenge in equal measure.

'Gifted' pupils excel in academic areas such as Maths, English, Science or Information Technology, whereas 'Talented' pupils are those who have special ability in Art, Dance, Music, Drama, Physical Education and Dance.

In their publication called 'Providing for Gifted and Talented Pupils', produced in December 2001, Ofsted say that:

'.....no school can say it has no gifted and talented pupils. An obvious consequence is that the composition of the gifted and talented population is likely to vary.....Pupils regarded as gifted and talented in one school may not be considered so in another school, whose intake of pupils is dissimilar'.

CHARACTERISTICS OF GIFTED AND TALENTED PUPILS

SPECIFIC AREA OF ABILITY	CHARACTERISTICS OF PUPIL
Intellectual ability in one or more subjects	Good memory and wide general knowledge; High level reading skills; Exceptional skills of deduction, reasoning and abstraction; Rapid thought processes.
Logical deductive thinking	Sees pattern and generation in complex tasks; Structured approach to problem solving; Tests hypotheses
Creative and lateral thinking	Flexibility; Originality of thought; Original ways of solving complex tasks; Plays with language, symbols and ideas; Processes information easily.
Interpersonal skills	Relates confidently with others; Self awareness and sensitivity; Demonstrates curiosity and interest in other people; Works independently; Good communicator and performer.
Skills of visualisation	Artistic and designs skill, including patter, form and function.
Physical ability	High levels of co-ordination and physical awareness.
Musical ability	Learns musical instruments rapidly; Good skills of composition; Confident performer.

PARENTAL ASSESSMENT:

For the purposes of this book, your own assessment as a parent will probably have led you to think of your child as more able in certain areas of life, such as quickness of learning or showing a marked aptitude in a particular field. What you want for your child is to be happy and fulfilled and if your child is intelligent, then his or her needs will need meeting. The table on the following page helps to identifiy the seven intelligences and then looks at how opportunities can be created to ensure that the child's ability flourishes.

GARDNER'S 7 INTELLIGENCES

INTELLIGENCE	CHARACTERISTICS	STRENGTHENING ACTIVITIES
LINGUISTIC Language	Articulate Selects vocab and word choices carefully Reads, writes and spells easily	Debates Discussion Letter writing Book reviews Word games and puzzles
LOGICAL- Mathematical Problems	Sees patterns and rhythms Sequences Puzzles Investigates	Number awareness Problem solving strategies Classifying and sorting Predicting and experimenting Reasoning
VISUAL SPATIAL Creative	Draws Follows directions Musical Good with maps and charts Thinks in pictures Constructs and designs	Art/sculpture/design Tessellation/patterns Concept mapping Interpreting and illustrating Using imagination and fantasy
BODILY Kinaesthetic Physical	PE and games Drama and movement Sense of touch Likes to manipulate objects May fidget and find it difficult to sit still	Drama, mime and role play PE and Dance Field trips Hands on learning Action rhymes
MUSICAL	Sensitive to pitch, tone and rhythm Aware of instruments Good sound discrimination	Use raps and chants to aid memory Use of music to enhance learning Rhythm activities
INTERPERSONAL Collaborative	Makes friends easily Teamwork Perceptive of others' feelings Organises others easily Communicates well	Collaborative working Peer tutoring Team games Circle time Group discussion and projects Conflict resolution activities
INTRAPERSONAL Personal	Identifies own emotions Knows strengths and weaknesses Self motivated	Autobiographical writing Personal goal setting Circle time study skills Self evaluation

Much of the stimulation and interest for more able children can be self-generated. From an early age bright children will respond to the stimuli which you as parents provide, and then generate their own interest. Seeing the child's interest, the parent often produces more challenging toys of interest and so a pattern of stimulus and response begins.

CHARACTERISTICS OF THE VERY ABLE AND TALENTED PRE-SCHOOL CHILD

What are some of the characteristics of the very able or talented pre-school child?

- ► Intense concentration, 'in a world of their own'
- ► Persistent behaviour, sometimes verging on the obsessional
- ► Unusual retentive memory
- ► Eagerness to learn, i.e. reading very early that seems to arise naturally – not from 'teaching' or coaching
- ► Talking very early
- ► More than the usual number of questions for a young child
- ► Telling jokes that peers do not find funny
- ► Very energetic, enthusiastic, curious and demanding
- ► Demonstrating an understanding of abstract concepts and complex relationships and categories and properties of objects earlier than is usual
- ► Talent in one particular area i.e. an understanding of number relationships and concepts

GETTING HELP FROM YOUR CHILD'S SCHOOL

All schools in the state sector now have to account for how they differentiate in interest and in the curriculum, for the more able child. Each school will have an assigned 'Gifted and Talented' co-ordinator who will be responsible for helping you with any queries about your child's needs.

- ► DO contact the co-ordinator, class teacher, subject teacher, Head of Year or Head teacher to discuss your child's needs and progress.
- ► Most schools will welcome discussions with parents and those who don't can be gently reminded about the Government initiative for more able children, which states that the needs of these children should be met within the school system.
- ► Local authorities also have someone who is responsible for more able children and this person will be contactable either on the LEA website or by telephone.

Is my child
above average?

IQ tests have their uses but, as a parent, you will want to make your own assessment before deciding to spend time and money on a professional statement. There are plenty of signs of above average intelligence that will be apparent to anyone who knows a child well. More able children have certain behaviour patterns in common and can be spotted by the way they do things. In other words: 'If it quacks, swims and waddles when it walks, then you can bet it's a duck.' The following quiz will give you a pretty good idea whether your child is one of the more able. It covers most of the traits that you would expect such a child to exhibit. The maximum score is 125.

▶ **To each of the statements below you should award marks as follows:**

Strongly disagree	Disagree	Not sure	Agree	Strongly agree
1	2	3	4	5

MY CHILD

1. Learned to read and write early

2. Possesses superior powers of reasoning

3. Has great intellectual curiosity

4. Enjoys playing with ideas

5. Frequently asks questions

6. Asks 'philosophical' questions (eg, What happens when people die?)

7. Shows keen powers of observation

8. Reads a lot

9. Is fascinated by computers

10. Is good at working with numbers

11. Has a large vocabulary including 'difficult' words

12. Is capable of great concentration

13. Can change from one activity to another very quickly

14. Has a wide range of interests

15. Can find it hard to relate to children of the same age

16. Makes frequent use of the internet as a research tool

17. Has a good memory

18. Can work independently

19. Can be bored with working in a team

20. Has a very good imagination

21. Can understand new ideas easily and quickly

22. Has been diagnosed as dyslexic

23. Has a powerful imagination

24. Finds school work boring and pointless

WHAT WAS YOUR SCORE?

95–125 A child who scores at this level is almost certainly very able

70–94 It is quite likely that your child is very able

50–69 Your child is probably of above average intelligence

Below 50 The signs of ability are not obvious but it is worth seeing how the child responds to the questions later in the book.

Common problems
and some solutions

 Just as doctors can list the ten most common ailments they are asked to treat, there are some very common problems with which parents of very able children need help. These same themes turn up again and again. They are set out here with some possible answers.

BOREDOM AND FRUSTRATION

Able children, especially very young ones, often find the school curriculum boring. If you've been able to read fluently since pre-school days you won't find the content of basic readers very gripping. At one time it was not the policy to let children forge ahead and read at their own pace. Some readers may remember the passage from *To Kill a Mockingbird* where Scout gets into trouble on her first day at school for being able to read fluently. Her teacher sends a message home that her father should stop teaching her because he doesn't know how to do it properly. Nowadays parents are likely to get more sympathetic treatment. It can be hard to get people to believe that your four-year-old doesn't merely need to read a more advanced book in the early reader series but actually needs proper books. Once the situation becomes clear you are likely to find that your child will be allowed to read something that is actually interesting.

Wherever possible bright kids should be allowed to work at their own speed. If they are forced to plod along at the speed of the class it's a bit like making a race horse pull a milk cart. If that happens children get frustrated and start to misbehave. If I had a penny for every time a parent has said to me: 'They say my kid is just naughty,' I'd be able to take early retirement. Gifted kids who are frustrated and not allowed to study at their own pace can become problem children. If you are in charge of them then, for the sake of your own sanity and theirs, you need to keep them interested.

BEING DIFFERENT

Unfortunately letting gifted kids work at their own pace solves one problem only to create another. Other children will quickly notice that the bright child is getting special treatment. A child may be allowed to give up basic readers and read a book about dinosaurs instead. The other kids, though not able to read the dinosaur book themselves, see that this book looks much more interesting than their books and want to know why one of their number is getting special treatment. The teacher explains that they, too, will have the chance to read more interesting books just as soon as they can manage them.

You have to face early on that a more able child is different and always will be. We accept all sorts of other differences (hair colour, personality, ability at sports, appreciation of music, etc) and it's important that high intelligence is seen as just another of those differences. No one pretends that this is easy.

Bright kids do still tend to get picked on but it is possible, slowly and carefully, to change attitudes. Nowadays most kids accept that it is wrong to make offensive remarks about someone's race, or to draw attention to another kid's disability. Eventually we will get to a stage where able children are seen as being different in a totally acceptable way.

TOTAL CONCENTRATION VERSUS BUTTERFLY MINDS

Intelligent kids have two modes of operation: they are capable of fiendish concentration when sufficiently interested in what they are doing but, on the other hand, they are easily bored, insatiably curious and inclined to let their minds flit about, investigating as many new things as possible. Both modes have their problems. The super-concentration can lead to the child remaining fiercely engrossed in a book when the class is supposed to be doing maths. It will take all the teacher's powers of persuasion to convince the child that it might be useful and interesting to study the whole curriculum.

The butterfly mind syndrome is more worrying because it is often confused with Attention Deficit Hyperactive Disorder (ADHD). This confusion has sometimes led to serious consequences such as perfectly healthy kids being dosed with the stimulant Ritalin that is used to treat ADHD. (For details on the problems of using Ritalin, go to http://www.breggin.com/ritalinconfirmingthehazards.html). Medical professionals, however, are increasingly aware of the hazards of mis-diagnosis.

There is a huge difference between a child who can't concentrate and one who doesn't want to. Also you have to be aware that gifted kids can appear not be concentrating while actually taking in every word. Before trying to 'treat' a child's apparent lack of concentration, it is important to establish exactly what is happening. One teacher told me about a girl in her science class who was known to be very bright indeed. She always gave the impression that her mind was on other things. She'd gaze out of the window or doodle. However, on several occasions when the teacher asked, 'What did I just say?' she got a detailed and correct answer. Eventually she accepted that the information was being absorbed, albeit in a rather unconventional way.

Do bright children
have pushy parents?

One of the criticisms levelled at families with more able children is that the parents are 'pushy'. By this people mean that a child who may be of only slightly above average intelligence is being forced by the parents into trying to become a prodigy. It also implies that the parents are putting pressure on the school to give their child special treatment.

ASSESSING THE PARENTS

Some parents are pushy. We have all come across the education junkies who move mountains (not to mention moving house) to make sure that their kid goes to the best schools, gets the top grades, and finally gets sent to one of the best universities as a preparation for a high-flying career.

But to find that you have a very able child is not like getting an unexpected Christmas present or a win on the lottery. It is often a difficult and even traumatic experience. Parents who are finding it distressing may need reassurance. People like this are almost certainly genuine. People who sound smug about having an exceptional child are usually pushy parents. I don't get many calls from people like that simply because they don't need advice: they already know exactly what they want and how to get it.

What leaves parents frustrated and depressed is that once you have a more able child it is easy to feel you are on your own. Many parents get the impression that their child is being treated as a freak and they are being blamed in some way for producing such an oddity. It is amazing how much comfort they take from being told: 'Yes, you have a perfectly normal, very able child. Most of them do the same things yours does. They generally turn out all right in the end.' This may seem a bit bland (and it is not the sum total of the advice they get), but it is the thing parents most need to hear. They can go back to their domestic situation feeling that they are no longer alone and misunderstood.

THE EXCEPTION TO THE RULE

One of the most dramatic examples in the UK is Ruth Lawrence, who at a very early age was seen to be a maths prodigy in the making. Her father took over her life and her education completely. Her academic progress was such that she was given a place at Oxford University when she was only 12. Her father accompanied her and the pair of them came in for quite a lot of criticism for the way in which he would egg her on to ask awkward questions during student debates. Eventually his domination of her life became more than she could take and there was a rift between them. Ruth Lawrence is now a highly respected academic. It seems her memories of her upbringing are not too rosy. In a newspaper interview she was reported as saying: 'I will not put my son through the hothouse training used to get me into Oxford when I was only 12. I want my Yehuda to have a childhood, not be forced to be different.'

DO INTELLIGENT PARENTS HAVE BRIGHT OFFSPRING?

Parents who are themselves highly intelligent have the advantage that they at least have personal experience of the problems and, though they might not have all the answers, they are familiar with the territory. But there is no rule that says that able kids can only be born to highly intelligent parents. There is a genetic component but it does not necessarily show itself all the time. It is quite common to come across parents who are in no way exceptional who nonetheless have produced a very bright child.

Having a bright child is great, but having one who is exceptionally intelligent can be very hard indeed. First, they have a need for constant attention and mental stimulation. As soon as they can talk they start to ask tough questions which get even tougher as they get a bit older. Then, when they finally get to school, the teachers are not always thrilled to have them. Teachers who are not equipped to deal with highly intelligent children often handle the situation by denying that the child is very bright. Instead they may say that the child is naughty or disruptive and does not get on with his or her peers. They may recognise the ability but may not be prepared to deal with it. The teacher's attitude can also infect the other parents who, when they get to hear about what is going on, blame the bright child for disrupting the class and damaging their own child's education. You can now see why, by the time parents seek help, they are often in a bad way. You can also see why no one in their right mind would want to push their child into such a situation.

A question
of class

 Is it true that able children are mainly middle-class? There is no doubt that plenty of highly intelligent kids are born into poorer families. The reason they don't get as much attention as they should is that these families are having a tough time to survive economically and they are therefore less likely to notice or value intelligence for its own sake.

THE MIDDLE CLASS

In middle-class families it is much more likely that the parents will not only notice the child's ability but will realise that they need to do something about it. But then something odd happens. Middle-class people tend to be intelligent, articulate and educated. They are used to being well treated by the system and being able to find ways to get what they want from it. Then they have an exceptional child and suddenly the system no longer supports them. They look to the school for support and may find ambivalence about what to do with the very able child. They don't get much sympathy from other parents either. They look around for people like themselves who might give help and support but they don't find any. It is this feeling of abandonment and isolation that causes many families real distress.

Can you improve
a child's intelligence?

Is it possible to boost someone's IQ? The answer is both yes and no. Psychologists agree that after maturity (at roughly age 16) intelligence doesn't increase. However, to quantify intelligence we have to rely on tests that are, in essence, just another type of exam. There have been many attempts to produce tests that measure pure intelligence without the waters being muddied by other considerations. Tests such as Raven's Matrices are specially constructed to be equally fair to people of all cultures. One version of Raven's is used for children because success in the test does not depend on acquired knowledge.

RAVEN'S TEST

The Raven's test works like this. Each page looks a bit like a sheet of patterned wallpaper with a swatch missing. Below are half a dozen swatches that might fill the hole but only one will complete the pattern correctly. The early puzzles are quite easy (a page filled with triangles can only be completed by a swatch marked in triangles, for example). Later, of course, the logic needed becomes more difficult.

If you do enough IQ tests you will eventually get good at them and you will be able to improve your score, so that it appears you have become more intelligent. Does this matter? Not really. If you have the intelligence and persistence to use this route to a higher score then you probably deserve the extra marks it gives you.

UK TV presenter Carol Vorderman revealed that when she got the job as the 'Numbers Girl' on Channel 4's cult puzzle programme Countdown, she found that her predecessor had been a Mensa member and the press insisted on reporting, quite inaccurately, that she was also a Mensan. She thought the best thing to do was to join, so she bought every book of IQ-type tests she could find and boned up on them until she could do the things in her sleep. It worked – she not only joined but was, for a while, a director of British Mensa. Whether she would have passed without all that preparation is something we will never know – though my guess is that she would have walked it, even if she had never touched an IQ test in advance.

The one thing you will never do, no matter how much you try, is to make a child of low or average IQ into a gifted child. That doesn't mean you shouldn't encourage all children to attain the utmost of which they are capable. All of us can, with a bit of effort, surprise ourselves by what we achieve.

Common sense is not so common.

Voltaire

What do we tell
the children?

Our forebears had the odd idea that we should never praise a child to his or her face. It was supposed to result in bigheadedness. Nowadays we believe in offering children all the encouragement we can and, especially, we like to praise them for their successes. Our attitude is that children are at far less risk of becoming conceited than they are at becoming discouraged by failure and criticism. But when it comes to bright kids, there are still those who feel that letting them know how clever they are will encourage them to adopt a superior attitude to their less intelligent peers. People who believe this sort of stuff don't know much about kids. If they did, they would realise that in any group of youngsters everyone knows who is bright, who is stupid (yes, children can be very blunt and are not good at political correctness), who is rich, who is poor, and who is best at sports. Kids regard this sort of knowledge as basic and are both surprised and contemptuous when adults try to obscure the truth.

RAW INTELLIGENCE

The best thing to do with able kids is to let them know exactly how bright they are but explain to them that raw intelligence is nothing to be proud of by itself. What matters is what they do with the abilities they've got. It is also as well to explain to them that people who are really bright don't go around showing off to others. A bit of modesty goes a long way in persuading people around you that you are an OK kind of person to be friends with.

I have come across families where being intelligent was regarded as the be all and end all of existence. They spent all their time doing 'intelligent' things and comparing their wonderful abilities with those of others who were not as bright. Guess what? These people never actually achieved anything worthwhile and no one ever really liked them. This should not come as a surprise.

10 misconceptions
about bright kids

There are a number of commonly held beliefs about gifted children that are either untrue or only partially true. It is important for a deeper understanding of such children to go through them one by one:

1 THESE KIDS ALL SUFFER BURN OUT IN LATER LIFE

The burn-out myth is a common one and is based on the bizarre notion that a child whose intellect is highly developed must be under some sort of mental strain. At the root of this belief lie two ideas. First, people who are not highly intelligent find mental work strenuous and assume that people who perform such work constantly must suffer a proportionate strain. Second, there is the envy factor. Because bright children seem to have an initial advantage over others, it must be paid for in later life by a compensating disadvantage. The truth is that bright children turn into bright adults who eventually become bright old people. They don't find being highly intelligent a strain: it is completely natural to them. You might as well ask whether a crab gets fed up with walking sideways. You only have to look at history: Albert Einstein, Isaac Newton, Galileo, and Leonardo Da Vinci all led long, productive lives with no sign of burning out.

2 THEY ARE BOOKWORMS WHO SPEND ALL THEIR SPARE TIME READING

It's true that bright kids are attracted to study. They enjoy understanding concepts that other people find complex and difficult. This doesn't mean that they aren't interested in the same things as other kids. Just because they find physics interesting it doesn't mean that they don't like rock music and if they decide to learn Ancient Greek in their spare time it doesn't mean they don't like going shopping with their friends. One of the most enthusiastic party-goers I have known had a secret passion for dinosaurs but she didn't let it take over her life. To able children, studying is as natural as playing football is to other kids. Of course there are always going to be some kids who are reclusive and lack social skills but this is not because they are highly intelligent – you can easily find plenty of children of much lower intelligence who are also reclusive. (There can be all sorts of reasons for reluctance to associate with other kids and these reasons need to be hunted down and dealt with.)

3 THEY ARE ALL COMPUTER GEEKS WHO HAVE NO LIFE OUTSIDE CYBERSPACE

Of all the beliefs about gifted kids this is the one that comes closest to being true. They do tend to be attracted to computers. It seems to have something to do with the fact that a computer is fast enough to keep up with the rate at which they think. For example, bright kids – especially boys – often have indifferent handwriting. I have always thought it was a sign of sheer frustration that they cannot express themselves in writing as quickly as they would like to. You can rattle away on a computer as fast as you like and these days it will even correct your spelling for you as you write. Kids are often fascinated by computers and get a lot of fun out of learning to work with them. It is not unusual to find young children who are already highly accomplished at programming. Working with computers gives them the chance to work in an area that gives them endless stimulation. Admittedly a few will turn into the sort of geeks who hide away in their bedroom for years with only their computer for company but these really are a tiny minority.

4 THEY ARE UNATTRACTIVE

The idea that bright kids look goofy and wear strange unfashionable clothes is completely untrue. A lot of the blame for this can be laid at the doors of the media. To take just one tiny example, think of the nerdy kids in 'Sabrina the Teenage Witch'. All the brainy kids are portrayed as ugly, unfashionably dressed and wearing really bad spectacles. They also have nerdy conversations about science. This is supposed to be humour but a lot of people really feel that this is the way gifted kids are. I've worked with literally hundreds of them and have found them on the whole to be attractive both in looks and personality. Their intelligence often shows in their expression. It is a look you grow to recognise and it makes them seems more rather than less attractive. Geena Davis, Jodie Foster and Sharon Stone are all known to be highly intelligent women. Need I say more?

5 THEY ARE NO GOOD AT SPORTS

This is a popular fallacy. Bright kids are no more or less likely to be bad at sports than the average youngster of their age. Some of them like sports and some don't, just like everyone else.

6 THEY ARE LONERS WHO ARE BAD AT RELATING TO THEIR PEERS

This is by no means always true but this has been known to happen. Able kids soon become aware that a lot of the things they think about are not appreciated or understood by their peers. Many of them are adept at fitting in with those around them. In some cases this even leads to bright kids deliberately underachieving so that they won't be labelled as 'brainy'. Some gifted children do let on how bright they are and this can be a mistake. There will always be children who feel that it's okay to pick on bright kids and make their lives a misery. What bright kids need most is contact with others who are as clever as themselves. If they have a place where it is safe for them to be themselves, they will be able to play the game of appearing 'normal' when they need to.

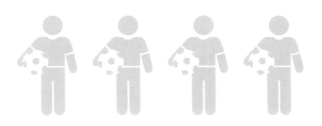

7 THEY HAVE 'WEIRD' IDEAS AND INTERESTS

Part of being highly intelligent is a desire to explore the world in every way possible. Such kids are interested in an enormous variety of subjects. They can be restless and will flit from one area of interest to another in search of something to satisfy them. They are not especially drawn to weird subjects, but if they see something that interests them, they are unlikely to be put off investigating just because other people consider the subject strange. Most of the great developments in science, art and many other fields of human endeavour were regarded as weird or even plain crazy before they were recognised as beneficial innovations.

8 THEY DON'T RESPECT THEIR ELDERS

All kids go through that teen stage where they question and rebel against adult authority. With able children there are a couple of things you need to remember. Never use the argument 'I'm older than you and therefore know best'. Reason with them the way you would with an intelligent adult and you'll find that, though they may still use you to vent their teenage angst, they will in time come to value you as someone they respect and trust.

9 THEY GO BONKERS IN THE END

Some able children will experience mental illness in their lives but so will huge numbers of people with less intelligence. There is no evidence to suggest that bright people are any more prone to such troubles than others. In fact there is reason to suppose that the reverse may the case – that highly intelligent people are better equipped to understand mental problems and get help in curing them. In particular they are often quite good at having insight into their own condition and learning to cope with it. This is part of the principle behind Cognitive Behavioural Therapy, which is flavour of the month right now for treating mental disorders. It depends very much on the patient having enough intellect and insight to be able – with help – to analyse and correct his or her own thought patterns.

10 THEY ARE TOO SERIOUS AND DON'T HAVE ANY FUN

Don't you believe it! If bright kids have a problem it is rather that their sense of fun is overdeveloped (especially when they get together). Although they are capable of obscure 'intellectual' witticisms they can also take delight in devilish practical jokes or sudden outbursts of sheer mayhem.

Teaching bright children:
problems and opportunities

Let's face it – teaching gifted kids is very hard work. The word demanding doesn't even begin to cover the sort of strain they place on their teachers. To make matters worse they are rare enough to make it hard for any teacher to gain experience of working with bright children. Below are some of the problems and some suggested tactics for dealing with them. The one golden rule is always to talk to able children as you would to intelligent adults, even when they are behaving badly. If you respect their intelligence, the chances are they will respect yours. The ideas below are not just for those in a formal teaching role. Any adult who wants to work with able kids needs to take what follows on board.

BE PREPARED FOR ENDLESS QUESTIONS

Normally teachers regard healthy curiosity as a good thing, but gifted kids can take it to extremes. Not only do they tend to hijack a class with endless queries but they regularly try to derail the whole lesson by pressing for information about what interests them rather than sticking to the subject at hand. Teachers are not superhuman and there is a limit to what they know. Having a child cross-question you about quantum mechanics when you are trying to explain photosynthesis can be very trying.

There are two ways of dealing with this. The bad way is to get impatient and tell the child to shut up. Even if this works (and it might not) you have now created an antipathy that won't make your relationship with the child any easier in the future. The better way is to agree that the question is interesting but point out this is not the place to discuss it. You can then promise to research some sources of further information for them. This often works. What the child wanted was not so much an immediate answer but for someone to show an interest.

By the way, if you live in the UK, you may find the 'Any Questions Answered' service a lifesaver. Just text your question to 63336 and they guarantee to find the answer, usually in a few minutes. The service costs £1 per question and is excellent value. I have been bowled over by their ability to dig up obscure bits of information that I have sought without success for ages. In the US there is a similar service available online. Answering 'I don't know' to a gifted child should always be followed by, 'How can we find out?'

EXPECT UNCONVENTIONAL ANSWERS

You never know what a gifted child will say next. Sometimes he or she gives an answer that leaves the teacher nonplussed. You may remember the scene in Jodie Foster's film 'Little Man Tate' where young Fred Tate's teacher writes some numbers on the board and asks which of them can be divided by 2. Fred seems to be showing no interest so she picks him to answer. He glances briefly at the board and says: 'All of them.' What the teacher really wanted to know was which of the numbers could be divided by two with no remainder. Having made one mistake she compounded it by looking flustered and a bit resentful. Bad move! When outsmarted by a gifted child you have to say, 'Well done, I didn't see that one coming!' Complete honesty will win you respect and future co-operation. Bluster and resentment will create an enemy of a potential friend.

DON'T BE SURPRISED IF ABLE CHILDREN DON'T SHOW INTEREST IN THE SYLLABUS

Teachers are supposed to guide their pupils through a course of study, making sure that they jump all the right fences on the way. There is a certain body of knowledge the students are expected to acquire and they are supposed to demonstrate their proficiency by producing course work and passing exams. So what happens if one child in the class decides that he hates history and wants to use the time to study astronomy instead? Not only does the teacher not have the time, resources and knowledge to co-operate but his success as a teacher depends

entirely on getting the children to do what the education authority demands of them.

Teachers often fail to understand one of the basics of dealing with bright kids. You don't educate them: you simply offer help and encouragement while they teach themselves. This will be troublesome and frustrating but as long as that child is in your class that is how things are going to be. There are two options. One is to simply let the child go his or her own sweet way, as long as this doesn't upset the rest of the class. The other is to explain to the child that, although you fully understand his or her desire to learn about things that interest them, there are some real advantages to toeing the line and passing exams. This often works. I know any number of gifted kids who were (eventually) persuaded to buckle down and get good grades so that they could go to the university they wanted to.

WATCH OUT FOR DISTRACTION TECHNIQUES

When intelligent children are prepared to stick to the syllabus they cover the ground much faster than their peers, leaving plenty of spare time to distract others and get into mischief. One solution is to set them extra work on the same topic to fill their time. But when they aren't even trying to do the work expected of them, they have even more time available for devilment. Many able children love to think up ingenious ways to cause mayhem. Teachers cannot ignore blatant rule breaking just because the perpetrator is highly intelligent, but it makes sense for the punishment to fit the crime. Getting the

miscreant to write an essay on the theme of crime and punishment is much more productive than merely handing out a detention. Whenever possible, use opportunities to get the kids to analyse their own behaviour in relation to those around them. The advantage of being highly intelligent is that they can be surprisingly honest and perceptive in their assessment of themselves.

PRESENTATION ISN'T IMPORTANT TO ABLE KIDS

Teachers, particularly those teaching younger children, are keen on neat, tidy work that is well presented. Intelligent kids are often very poor at this. My theory is that they think so quickly that trying to translate it all into writing becomes a strain. They are interested in the ideas for their own sake and find the business of getting them down on paper intensely frustrating. Teachers often misinterpret this as deliberate indiscipline. Some teachers even use scruffy presentation as a proof that the child, far from being gifted, is somewhat below average. The assumption is that an able child could produce neat, tidy work if he or she tried harder. This is mistaken. From my experience I would suggest that many, if not most, gifted kids (especially boys) simply can't do neat and tidy even if they try hard. However, once they are allowed to express themselves on a computer they tend to blossom and produce very creative, highly articulate work. The teacher's best option is to get an able child to a computer as soon as possible. A lap-top computer can be used effectively.

BE PREPARED FOR THE PARENTS TO WANT TO TALK

The parents of gifted children can be under a great deal of stress. They feel others fail to understand exactly what they are going through. If they seek meetings with teachers to discuss their problems, they often find that there is little help to be had. The school may simply not have enough resources to provide for a child who needs a lot of personal attention. Lack of resources is a problem that cannot easily be solved. However, there are many ways that a gifted child can be helped outside school through clubs, 'enrichment' activities and on-line activities. Schools should have a Gifted and Talented Co-ordinator to point parents in the right direction.

LOOK OUT FOR DIFFERENCES BETWEEN ABLE CHILDREN AND THEIR PEERS

Some bright kids find it hard to make friends with 'normal' children of their own age. They tend to use words that other kids don't know and they talk about ideas that sound strange. And they may have a sense of humour that goes over the heads of their peers. Young children are great conformists and as they reach the teenage years the desire to belong gets stronger. They make a great effort to be just like everyone else and censor anyone who is obviously different. If in addition to being 'weird' a child is also very clever (and kids are much better than teachers at knowing who is intelligent), then there will also be an element of jealousy mixed in with the general disapproval. All

this can lead to isolation or even bullying. There is no quick fix. Parents need to explain to able children that that just because they know and understand more than other people, that is no reason to rub their noses in it. The message is: enjoy your abilities but don't flaunt them. With luck others will accept you with good grace, just as they would if you were top at sports.

ABLE CHILDREN AREN'T ALWAYS TEAM PLAYERS

We live in the age of the team. Look down the Situations Vacant column of any newspaper and you will find that being a team player is regarded as essential for many jobs. Instead of talking about managers, we now call them team leaders and many companies hold exercises that are meant to instil team spirit in employees. Schools are expected to produce kids who have the right attitude to the team. Able kids frequently don't do team spirit. They can't see the point of working with a crowd of people who think at a plodding pace and who concern themselves with trivialities when they could be doing something interesting. If they're sensible they probably won't say any of these things out loud, but their lack of enthusiasm will become evident.

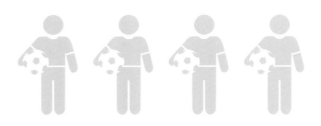

RESPECT ISN'T AUTOMATIC

Some adults have the idea that children owe them respect simply by virtue of age difference. This is a dumb idea at the best of times and when you're dealing with gifted kids, it is simply absurd. If you want respect you'll have to go and earn it. Because they can think at an adult level (and we are talking here about the level of a very smart adult), able kids tend to treat adults with familiarity. This can be disconcerting but, if you let yourself get used to the idea, it can also be refreshing. Discussing, arguing, and laughing (not to mention occasionally quarrelling) with gifted kids will do them and you nothing but good. If you can pit your wits against them and gain respect you'll have achieved something worthwhile. If you resort to yelling, 'Do as I tell you!' then you will be the poorer for it.

> **If the human brain were so simple that we could understand it, we would be so simple that we couldn't.**
> *Emerson M. Pugh*

Bright kids cannot be treated like a national resource

Sometimes you hear educationalists talk about bright kids as a national resource. They talk them up as the intellectual high fliers of tomorrow who will lead their nation in the paths of prosperity and intellectual excellence. Politicians have caught on to this too and, since it has resulted in investment in education of bright children, the notion is not bad in itself – it just happens to be untrue.

BRIGHT KIDS AS EXPLORERS

Bright kids are not like an oil reserve: you can't gather them in, refine them and then set them to work on tasks of national importance. Some may do this of their own accord but to act as though they can all be pressed into the service of the nation is foolish. Gifted kids will very often engage in things that may seem utterly useless, crazy or even dangerous. This is because all the really good new ideas are found by people who are prepared to think the unthinkable. They do not all end up producing anything of practical value but they do extend the sum of human knowledge and that is very, very important. As humans, our defining characteristic is that we are insatiably curious and able to engage in abstract thought that may or may not be of any practical use. The whole thinking process is very hit and miss. A lot of effort gets wasted in projects that eventually lead nowhere. But that is the nature of intellectual investigation and, as Edison famously reminded us, it can be just as important to know the things that don't work.

There is a perfectly understandable tendency amongst politicians to want to encourage, guide and even lure youngsters into areas that will be productive. After all, it takes a lot to educate kids and train them for employment and there is a feeling that the investment should yield a substantial return as soon as possible. The trouble is that we can never know with any certainty which areas will produce and which won't. Consider the benefits we have reaped from people who insisted on doing 'impossible' things only to find that they were not impossible after all.

We desperately need to encourage people of high intelligence to explore as widely and deeply as possible without being too concerned about what they find. We need this because it is what human beings are for. If they happen to discover the secrets of cold fusion or perpetual motion along the way, that is a bonus, but the endless search is vital.

Together
or apart?

Should bright kids be educated along with less able children or should they be kept separate and educated with their intellectual equals? This debate has been one of the great battlefields of modern education. There are a number of options that need to be considered separately.

SEPARATING CHILDREN BY ABILITY

People of a certain age will remember having been part of the streaming or tracking system. In each school all children of the same age were classified by intellectual ability and taught in separate groups. In its most brutal form the groups, streams or tracks were labelled A, B, C and D, so that you were in no doubt who were the bright kids and who were the least able. In some schools they attempted to disguise the truth by calling the groups by different, less divisive names. Was anyone fooled? No way. End of term exams were also used to rank children in order in each subject. The system has long been abandoned in this form. In the US, though, percentage scores in high school subjects are still part of the college admission process. Veterans of the top stream or track will no doubt reflect that the system served them well, but you cannot ignore students lower down.

MIXING ALL ABILITIES TOGETHER

The reaction against the old divisive system was so strong that it resulted in an equally stupid system based on total equality. The object was to give all children an equal chance by pitching them all into the same class regardless of ability. The theory was that the bright kids would stimulate the less able and everyone would benefit. This system still has its advocates. I was recently treated to an impassioned defence of mixed ability teaching from the principal of a local high school. Within a couple of days an article in one of the national dailies also made a case for mixed ability classes.

The argument against is that the children of lower ability often have no interest in learning anything and frequently manage to disrupt the class to the point where those who want to learn became discouraged and frustrated. If mixed ability teaching frustrates children of just above average ability, think what effect it has on those who are gifted. They sit there with their engines racing and nowhere to go.

It was to improve the situation that educationalists came up with another approach – sets or cluster groups. This approach is predominant in the more successful secondary schools and is being adopted more widely.

SIMILAR ABILITIES, DIFFERENT SUBJECTS

A set or cluster group consists of a number of children of similar ability who are taught together. This system has great advantages. It allows able children to work to their true level of ability, while less able kids can get help in areas where they are weak. It also caters for the fact that some kids are good at one subject but poor at another – a child might be in group 1 for Maths but group 3 for French. It also removes a lot of the stigma attached to being less able because the system is fluid and kids can be transferred from group to group as necessary. This is very important, because some children who find a subject difficult do eventually, after a bit of remedial help, 'get it' and can continue at a more advanced level. Only a tiny minority of children find themselves in bottom groups for everything. Currently setting or cluster grouping is popular with many teachers, children, and parents. It is obviously popular with gifted kids because it allows them to get on with study without being constantly mocked for their ability and enthusiasm.

TEACHING BRIGHT KIDS INDIVIDUALLY

Some schools are willing to take bright kids and let them work alone on material that is too advanced for their peers. This can help to stop the child from becoming bored but it places increased demands on the teachers, and not everyone is willing or able to make the effort. It can also separate bright children from their peers and result in them being labelled as different. But, as I have said elsewhere, there is no fooling children: they will already know that the bright child is clever

whether they are told or not, so, on balance, no great harm will be done. This system is a heavy drain on resources; a child is likely to be offered this sort of help only in one or two subjects that he or she excels at. To provide entirely separate teaching for one child would not only be too expensive but would have the entirely undesirable effect of separating the child completely from others.

SKIPPING A YEAR

Sometimes bright kids are moved up a class so that they are working in the company of older children on more advanced work. This is extremely unpopular with many schools and teachers. The argument is that while the child may have a higher mental age, his or her emotional development will not necessarily keep up. Many a bitter struggle has taken place between teachers and parents over whether a child should be advanced a year. Many more will no doubt take place in the future. There is no magical right answer to this dilemma. It depends on the character of the child, the willingness of the school and the attitude of the parents. From my own schooldays, when it was quite common to move gifted children up a year, I can remember several who seemed to manage in an older class perfectly well. In particular I recall one who, though a year younger than the rest of us, still regularly came top of the class. No one seemed to mind. Research in the US supports the idea that skipping a year or 'acceleration' is usually successful for bright kids. Acceleration by subject is also very common.

HOT-HOUSING OR ISOLATING BRIGHT KIDS

There are various types of education that come into this category. The most extreme form of hot-housing would be to gather a group of highly intelligent children together and educate them in isolation from those of lesser ability. As far as I know this has never been attempted in any systematic way. There were rumours during the Cold War that the Soviets did it but, of course, the information was not made public. The whole idea sounds a bit like science fiction. Would high IQ children who had experience only of others like themselves ever fit into the normal world? Gifted kids are perfectly normal and enjoy the same things as others of their age. I doubt that they would take very well to a life that consisted of little but accelerated learning. In the US dedicated schools for gifted kids do educate them in isolation but the children get plenty of opportunity to take join the local community in after-school activities.

Some parents set out to isolate and hot-house their own children. The most recent case is that of the maths genius, Sufiah Yusof, who was accepted by St Hilda's College, Oxford, when she was only 13. She ran away after her third year and blames her parents for years of 'physical and emotional abuse.' Such stories don't make hot-housing such an attractive proposition.

What a distressing contrast there is between the radiant intelligence of the child and the feeble mentality of the average adult.

Sigmund Freud

What do we do
with bright children?

Once very able kids have been found, identified and labelled, what do we do with them? You can't just release them back into the world like a rare species of butterfly, but there is considerable difference of opinion about what they actually need. Here are the main options:

GIVE THEM MORE OF THE SAME

Let's say that the child you've discovered shows signs of being a physics prodigy. It is tempting to give him or her some more advanced physics to do. Maybe, if you are lucky enough to have found more than one gifted physicist, you could hold some master classes in which they could be helped to explore their subject to a more advanced standard. This is fine but, given the lack of resources for such children, it might not be the best use of valuable time. Gifted kids have a knack of pursuing their own interests without much outside help. I can think of any number who reached a very high standard in their chosen discipline with little or no outside help. Their knack for tracking down the information they require is uncanny. They will also find other children of like mind of share and explore their subject.

ORGANISE ENRICHMENT ACTIVITIES

Enrichment has become a bit of an educational buzzword recently. It involves exposing children to ideas that are outside their normal experience. The new ideas can be almost anything as long as they are sufficiently unusual and interesting. For example, I came across a school where a member of staff was allowed to offer bright kids the chance to study Japanese or Chinese. Apart from the obvious usefulness of such languages there is also the fact that they involve not just novel vocabulary and grammar but whole new thought patterns quite unlike anything you find in western languages. This helped the kids understand that our own attitude to language is not the only one. They were amazed to discover that reading Chinese characters allowed complex thought patterns to be expressed very succinctly and read at high speed.

Enrichment is hugely valuable but it depends on having resources available and having enthusiastic adults who are willing to share their private enthusiasms with young people.

PUT THEM IN CONTACT
WITH OTHER BRIGHT KIDS

Apart from purely scholastic needs, the other really urgent requirement is for contact with other children like themselves. It is impossible to over-emphasise the importance of this. Very able children need to know that they are not freaks, not alone, and that there are people out there of their own age with whom they can communicate and make friends. They need to be able to speak freely without being teased because they have unusual interests. Already schools have been involved in events designed to bring their gifted pupils together and, having been involved in the organisation of some of these, I would be very happy to see the idea spread far and wide.

ONE OF A KIND

In 1911 a starving Native American was found wandering in the corral of a slaughterhouse in Oroville, California. At first people thought he was insane because he appeared to babble complete nonsense. Eventually it was discovered that his name was Ishi and he was the very last member of the Yana tribe. He was not crazy but spoke a language that he alone understood. Gifted children are not in quite such a desperate condition but, even so, are quick to see parallels with their own experience

The sense of relief they experience when this contact is made is wonderful to behold. The first time MFGC got 130 kids together for a day the effect was truly magical. It was as if our friend Ishi (see box) had suddenly stumbled upon a whole Yana village.

IS ANYONE OUT THERE?

The good news is that MFGC is going to establish a new email list by which gifted kids can contact each other. Full details are available by emailing mfgckids@fsmail.net There are various rules designed to keep kids safe but, apart from that, we want a free and easy environment where people will feel at home and will make new friends throughout the world.

What about
home schooling?

Most kids moan about school but in many ways they find it enjoyable. They meet their friends, catch up with the gossip, and get involved in activities they enjoy, such as sports, drama or music, which they simply couldn't do alone. Some of them will, if pressed, admit to enjoying at least part of the academic side of schooling. They will even tell you that some of the teachers are really cool. My daughter's art teacher gets regular visits from people who left the school years ago but still hold him in high regard and come back to let him know what they are doing and ask his advice.

WHO IS HOME SCHOOLING FOR?

Sadly there are always some kids who just never feel at home in school. It might be because they suffer from bullying but in some cases the whole education process just feels alien to them. They can't stand the atmosphere at school and find it makes them ill. Their parents may tell them that this is what life is like and they'd better get used to it. But if this has no effect, what next? If kids are forced to go to school they'll simply fake illness or play truant until they and their parents get into trouble with the authorities. Eventually the parents come round to the only alternative left – home schooling.

I'm sure there are parents reading this and saying, 'If she were my child I'd make her go to school all right!' But before you get too judgmental, you should read some of the letters and articles by children who have had to leave school in this way. No one could fail to have sympathy with their strange but serious plight.

The other class of home schoolers are the parents of kids who suffer from illness that makes attendance at school difficult or impossible. One of the ex-Bright Sparks has suffered for years from myalgic encephalitis or ME (which used to be known as 'yuppie flu') and continues her education in fits and starts whenever her illness allows. She was never formally home schooled but a lot of her education had to be done at home simply because she was too ill to get to school.

THE PROS AND CONS

Given the level of governmental control that exists, it's surprising that home schooling is still legal in the UK. The authorities may be awkward and try to make you re-join the system but, as long as you stick to the rules, there is nothing they can do to stop you. By contrast in the US, home schooling is becoming more and more popular and is often encouraged by education authorities. There are many reasons why you should keep your child in school. School provides more than just academic instruction, it also has facilities such labs, gyms, and workshops, that you couldn't provide at home. It also equips kids with social skills and a network of friends. (To counter these disadvantages in the US, home schoolers often get together and form their own social network.)

If you have ever tried to teach your kids anything at home (even something simple like telling the time), you will know that once parents are involved all sorts of emotional issues come into play. Teachers have a distance that allows them to work together in a less emotionally charged atmosphere.

Home schoolers are regarded by the rest of society as at best eccentric and at worst a little crazy. This may be an unkind view but it can contain a grain of truth. People who want to protect their children from the world at large may not be taking the right approach by isolating their children. Yes, there are things wrong with society but they aren't going to be put right by people who opt out.

There are some good things about home schooling. It allows parents to teach things that don't appear in the normal curriculum. In the UK, if you want your child to learn astrophysics, archaeology or Sanskrit then you are within your rights to include these in your curriculum. As long as you can show your child is getting a proper education you can teach anything you want. You can also teach attitudes and beliefs that you value. In the US the basic state curriculum is the minimum and extra subjects can be added to it.

The Useful Resources section gives details of organizations that can help. But before you go down this route, do think long and hard. It's a hard and bumpy road and your child's whole future is at stake.

What's going to happen to my child?

One of the questions that gets asked again and again by distraught parents is the one about what the future holds for a gifted child. What they are after is some reassurance that their child is capable of having a happy life. In most cases I've been able to say with a clear conscience: 'Yes, the chances are it will all turn out fine.' Once very able kids leave school, things get easier for them. Adults can be unkind to people who are different but, on the whole, they are not nearly as cruel as children. Adults are also able to recognise that, even though people may seem eccentric, it does not preclude them being useful. You hear comments like: 'Old Jim's a bit odd but you should have seen him work out that timetable. It would have taken me weeks but he got it finished in a day!' So let's look at the positive outcome we all hope for.

WHEN IT ALL GOES RIGHT

You don't hear much about intelligent people who are happy, and enjoy fulfilling careers. Why? Well, for the same reason that the media seldom bother to report good news. People are really only interested in hearing about bright people coming unstuck. A recent magazine devoted a four-page article to gifted people who'd come badly unstuck during their lives. Einstein?

Bad father, unfaithful husband. Michelangelo? Unsociable. Dirty. Probably autistic. Virginia Woolf? Mental breakdown at age 13 with others to follow. Eventual suicide. And that was less than half of the first two pages!

Why are the media so obsessed with the downside of giftedness? Partly because it makes better news. Another part of the answer is more complex. A lot of people resent cleverness. Intellectuals are seen as dangerous thinkers who set out to challenge the way things are done and to introduce new and revolutionary ideas. Most people rather enjoy the status quo (especially if it is operating in their favour socially and financially). So people who have the potential to cause major upsets are not viewed with much affection.

It would take only a matter of minutes to think of gifted children who turned out to be productive, happy adults but such a list wouldn't get published. The idea that bright children will turn out to be nerdy or maladjusted adults is almost an article of faith in some quarters. Only people who fit this profile will ever be put forward as example of what happens to bright children when they mature. It is one of those popular myths like the one that maintains that millionaires are lonely and miserable people whose lives have been destroyed by money. Any millionaires who happen not to fit that profile can be safely ignored.

There is a widespread feeling that no good can come of being very intelligent. I've spoken to many parents who found that once it was known their child was very bright then other parents would look askance at them and pass disagreeable remarks.

THE END RESULT

Many highly intelligent children do grow up to be happy adults. They will always, of course, be a bit different from their peers and some of them will be a trifle eccentric (which is not a crime), but there is no doubt at all that many of them are happy. Just look around and you'll find them in numerous professions, in government, in laboratories and a thousand other places. The reason they are not much noticed is this: once they finish their education no one really cares about their IQ any more. With luck they will discover a life that makes them happy, lose all interest in IQ and never find any reason to discuss it again. Once you know that you have a career and a life that you enjoy, why would you be at all interested in wondering whether you were intelligent enough to do it? It would be like Pavarotti wondering whether his voice was good enough. People who sit around and obsess constantly about their IQ level are the ones who have a problem. The IQ, as I never tire of saying, is meaningless in itself – you have to go and do something useful with it!

The first time I found a group of happy and useful high IQ people working together was when I was asked to be a consultant on a TV game show in which the ultimate prize would be a trip into space. I went along to the first session and was promptly bowled over with surprise. The people round the table were not only very bright but also humorous, well-adjusted, friendly and adept at working together in harmony. Even though I had always insisted that it was perfectly possible for gifted people to behave in this way, until then I would have had to admit that I'd never seen it happen.

When it all goes
horribly wrong

Apart from the obvious things that all children need, an able child needs two extra things: study that is suited to his or her abilities, plus some friends of a similar level of intelligence. As long as these things are available there is a good chance that the child will grow up to be a reasonably productive and well-adjusted adult. Of course, other factors may interfere (divorce or death of a parent, for example), but these are the same sort of disasters that may affect any child.

THE START OF A DOWNWARD SPIRAL

When a child's needs are not always met, that's when he or she can start to 'go wrong'. Several scenarios usually spell trouble. The first is where a child is discouraged by peers (and, occasionally, parents) from reaching his or her full potential. A child who is bullied at school may end up truanting to get away from an intolerable situation. Theoretically this shouldn't happen these days: there are school policies to prevent bullying and there are requirements for schools to provide appropriate education for gifted pupils. But just because something is required by regulations doesn't mean that the rules are always obeyed. Plenty of people still find gifted kids annoying and use them as an easy target. Recent research broadcast in the UK showed that even in schools with exemplary anti-bullying credentials the practice is almost impossible to stamp out. For at least part of the time children inhabit a world where adults are not admitted and it is very hard to find what goes on there.

There is another disturbing development. In spite of the fact that we are healthier and more prosperous than any people in history, we are by no means a happy breed. This applies as much to children as to their parents. There are plenty of depressed, disillusioned and hopeless people out there. If you have teenagers who talk to you then you will undoubtedly know of kids who self-harm, truant, take drugs or get wasted on booze. These are desperate problems for any child to cope with. Intelligent kids who are miserable don't suffer more, but they do tend to use their intelligence in ways that make matters worse. For example, I came across a piece of research done by a gifted teenager that listed a great variety of ways to commit suicide, together with the pros and cons. What was shocking was the detail he'd gone into.

ANYTHING CAN HAPPEN

When a gifted child's frustrations turn inwards, it is the child and the family who suffer. But what happens when the child directs its attention outwards? Almost anything can happen and you can bet that it will spell trouble. For example, Al Capone was known to have been highly intelligent; those who have met him, testify that Osama bin Laden is also in the high IQ category. Not all intelligent but unhappy people will turn out to be master criminals but there are many lesser ways in which aggrieved people can make others suffer. Of all the companies I have worked for in more than 30 years, the two that bring back shudders when I think of them are the ones in which very bright people were allowed to become bored, discontented or, worse still, were actively encouraged by their bosses to scheme and plot against each other. Given the opportunity, it is amazing just how much misery bright people will inflict on themselves and others. It is therefore in everyone's interest to identify able kids early and make sure that they get the sort of education that will help them become fulfilled and happy people who are willing to use their abilities for the good of everyone.

What most often happens to gifted people who don't get the right opportunities is not that they decide to take over the world but that they sink into a state of dissatisfied apathy and sullen resentment. This is typified by a remark I heard from a highly intelligent man who somehow had never been able to do better for himself than a low paid job as a truck driver. He looked grumpily at the head office of the company he worked for and muttered: 'Do you realise that everyone in there gets paid more than me apart from the cleaner?' It was a sad commentary from someone who had never been able to live up to his abilities.

Useful Resources

G&TWISE (FORMERLY XCALIBRE)
www.teachernet.gov.uk/gtwise
At the time of writing this, the content was not yet posted on this site, so we cannot comment on the navigation of the site or on its content. However, this should offer a searchable catalogue of G&T resources produced by a wide range of G&T organisations and recommended by those working in the G&T field.

G&TWISE
www.teachernet.gov.uk/gtwise or www.londongt.org
G&TWise is a new part of the TeacherNet website, designed to support all those involved in the education of the gifted and talented. From the end of March 2005, it will offer a searchable catalogue of G&T resources, produced by widely respected organisations in the field of education, such as London Gifted and Talented (LG&T) and the National Association for Able Children in Education (NACE).

DfES
www.standards.dfes.gov.uk/giftedand-talented
Apart from the standard DfES information there are some useful links to international sites. Some very useful good practice case studies. Very user-friendly and useful content.

LONDON GIFTED AND TALENTED
www.londongt.org
A useful calendar of events and opportunities for teachers and pupils. Beginnings of a very good collection of online materials. Call them to get a password and access all areas.

OXFORD BROOKES
www.brookes.ac.uk/schools/education/ablepupils/
Resources area still under construction. Very useful professional development materials which can be downloaded and links section good. User friendly.

NAGTY (WARWICK)
www.warwick.ac.uk/gifted/primary

For pupils and parents with a new section addressing the primary sector so it's worth keeping an eye on this site.

NATIONAL CURRICULUM GUIDANCE (QCA)
www.nc.uk.net/gt

Excellent subject specific and general guidance – great to print out for subject coordinators or teachers who have pupils with a specific need. Easy to navigate.

NAGC
www.nagc.org

Lots of useful background reading for teachers and parents. Need to be a member to access some areas of site eg resources.

NACE NATIONAL ASSOCIATION FOR ABLE CHILDREN IN EDUCATION
www.nace.co.uk

Great resources and many CPD opportunities. Lots of links to other sites.

WORLD COUNCIL FOR G&T CHILDREN
www.worldgifted.org

A list of worldwide resources, organisations and research.

EUROPEAN COUNCIL FOR HIGH ACHIEVERS
www.echa.ws

A continental perspective on provision for able pupils. This site includes a range of resources, research reports, articles, forums and an area for children in which they can question experts and enter competitions.

GIFTED READING
IS FUNDAMENTAL
www.rif.org.uk

Information on and interviews with authors, illustrators and poets plus book reviews, competitions and links to lots of other sites for keen readers.

READING CONNECTS
www.readingconnects.org.uk

A National Reading Campaign initiative that supports schools in using reading for pleasure to enhance achievement. Read practical ideas, developed by schools and key reading-related organisations, to encourage the reading habit. Share case studies, and a wide range of resources, as well as getting advice on funding to help you promote reading for pleasure.

NATIONAL LITERACY TRUST

www.literacytrust.org.uk/whatson/writingcomps

A regularly updated list of writing competitions. If you search more widely on this site, you will also find an enormous database of Literacy information and resources.

THE NEWSPAPER

www.thenewspaper.org.uk

A free national newspaper for 8 to 13-year-olds, with sections covering news, sport, celebrities, the environment, and science and technology, and space for the readers to try their hand at journalism. There is currently a waiting list for those wanting to subscribe and coverage is being extended in phases. The website provides an online, printable version of the paper as well as additional teaching resources.

WORLD CLASS TESTS

www.worldclassarena.org

Maths tests for very able mathematicians

NRICH ONLINE MATHS CLUB

www.nrich.maths.org

Bernard's bag is good for challenging able pupils, you have to join, but it's free.

WOGNUM

www.wognum.se

Click on brainwave for logic puzzles

CIRCA MATHS

www.circamaths.co.uk

Website for the fantastic circa maths comics, which more able pupils really enjoy.

SCIENCE MUSEUM

www.nmsi.ac.uk

An extremely comprehensive and informative website. Lots of interesting information for both students and teachers. Children can listen in on haddock calls, send emails, take part in quizzes and read up to date news on science and technology. There is information about events for teachers and INSET information. Very user friendly.

ASSOCIATION FOR SCIENCE EDUCATION

www.ase.org.uk

Some good lesson starters based on the science behind the news headlines. You can subscribe free to weekly updates (Science upd8).

Year 7+ challenges in 'red hot activities'

EXPLORATORIUM CALIFORNIA

www.exploratorium.edu

Webpages on how to make telescopes etc. Go to Explore, then Hands on Activities. Lots of good ideas covering a wide range of the curriculum. For students and teachers.

ENGINEERING INTACT

www.eng.cam.ac.uk/mmg/teaching/pete rstidwill/interact/teachers4

An interactive science and engineering website. For use by KS1,2 and 3 children. Covers all science modules.

HOW STUFF WORKS

www.howstuffworks.com

An enormous database of explanations to satisfy even the most curious of pupils.

CONCEPT CARTOONS FOR SCIENCE

www.conceptcartoons.com

These are a great tool for extending and challenging children's thinking in Science.

TALENTED

TALENT LADDER

www.talentladder.org

Very useful reading for the PE Coordinator: information about the talent support programme and national opportunities for talented athletes, advice on how to develop talent in PE, research.

TALENT MATTERS

www.talentmatters.org

The results of a research project from Leeds Met University: identification of talent in PE, provision ideas, learning outcomes for talented athletes, suggested quality standards for talented PE provision.

CREATIVE GENERATION

www.creativegeneration.co.uk

Guidance on identification and provision, with examples of good practice in many arts areas including drama, dance, art, music.

CREATIVE DRAMA

www.creativedrama.com

Some good ideas for developing children's talents.

THINKING SKILLS

DFES THINKING SKILLS

www.standards.dfes.gov.uk/think-ingskills

A good general overview and history of thinking skills with a resource database and case studies.

COGNITIVE ACCELERATION THROUGH SCIENCE EDUCATION (CASE)

www.case-network.org.uk

If you are interested in CASE, the Maths version (CAME) or the KS1 Let's Think! programmes, this site contains a lot of information about the research and theory as well as details of training (though it has a heavy CASE focus).

TEACHING THINKING

http://www.teachthinking.com

This is a quarterly magazine from Questions Publishing Company, Birmingham. It contains practical articles on a range of thinking skills approaches.

THE SOCIETY FOR THE ADVANCEMENT OF PHILOSOPHICAL ENQUIRY AND REFLECTION IN EDUCATION

http://www.sapere.net/

SAPERE is a small charitable organization that promotes the use of philosophical techniques and approaches in the classroom both as a model of rigorous thinking and as a celebration of wonder and open-mindedness. It is a member of the International Council for Philosophical Inquiry with Children.

ROBERT FISHER

www.teachingthinking.net

Robert Fisher is a prolific and successful author of many thinking skills titles for primary age pupils and also his Philosophy for Children book.

EDWARD DE BONO

www.edwdebono.com

Edward De Bono is an internationally renowned advocate of thinking skills. Find out all about him and his ideas on this site, and especially his Thinking Hats.

Index